ONE

TWO

The Anti-Book League

First published in 2017 by The Anti-Book League.

ISBN 978-1-910375-61-7

No words were harmed in the making of this book. All the events and characters described in it are real and any resemblance to fictional persons is purely coincidental.

CONTENTS

PREAMBLE

Once in several generations, somewhere in the world, comes a charismatic personality who has a profound effect on people's thinking. The subject of this short biographical sketch is not one of them. His life was ended before his mission had barely begun, and he died in exile and obscurity.

After years of abandonment, with the rent unpaid, an entry was forced into a lock-up garage in the town of Bognor Regis, West Sussex, England. It was established that the lessee had departed this world for an unknown destination and, with no relatives to be found, it was decided that the contents of the garage, whatever they might be, should be sold and the proceeds handed over to the landlord in lieu of unpaid rent. Inside was discovered a rusted moped, propped up on its stand above a dried-up pool of engine oil. Against one wall was a rack of metal shelving, dusty and begrimed, supporting bits and bobs of accumulated junk.

On one of the shelves sat, rather incongruously, a row of old books, the reason for me being there in my capacity as a second-hand bookseller. Among those volumes I later discovered a tatty notebook, filled with a few random jottings concerning the life of an inspirational revolutionary leader, written by his most devoted follower, who had rented the garage to store the sum of his worldly possessions. I made the decision to edit and publish what little there was in the notebook, in the hope that it might flush out further information concerning its unusual subject and perhaps induce an abler hand than mine to apply itself to penning a much fuller account of the man and the movement he wished to spread. Somewhere, there may even be diaries awaiting rediscovery.

Certainly, there must be eye-witnesses alive who could provide further testimony. Back in the day, communication was not so easy, but with the social media of modern times it is not inconceivable that fresh facts could yet be forthcoming.

It should be noted that the subject of this biographical piece did not *start* the revolution. He merely acted as a figurehead of his time and gave a name to the movement. Many revolutionaries preceded him, from the irrepressible Socrates to the Marx Brothers—Harpo, Chico, Groucho and Karl. Some of these influences were identified by the turned down corners of pages in the books found in the garage, a collection that had been inherited from the great leader himself. Others have followed too, although almost invariably acting independently. Perhaps some day the vision of the hero of this account, to have a united international revoltionary movement, will one day be realised. It is not a revolution that everyone will comprehend. As the man in question once said, 'If it has to be explained then it won't be understood.' Neither is it a revolution that can ever be *won*, but it will certainly *never be lost* while even a few remain true to the cause.

Finally, on a technical point, the author of the original manuscript was in the habit of placing random full stops ('periods' to our American brethren) in the middle of. sentences, a practice that, for the sake of convenience, I do not intend to. replicate in the following transcription.

A Citizen

THE END

As dawn broke on the first day of April, 1974, an Englishman was escorted across a South American military courtyard and tied by the waist to a wooden stake. Facing him was a firing squad, bedecked in full dress uniform of braided tunics and plumed shako caps. Standing to one side was the commanding officer, who proceeded to address the prisoner.

'Have you any last request? A cigarette, perhaps?'

The prisoner shook his head.

'I'm trying to quit.'

The officer bowed respectfully.

'I wish you success, Señor.'

He lifted his ceremonial sword high above his head as a signal for the soldiers to raise and cock their weapons. Then, as he cut down through the air with a terrific *swoosh*, the crack of rifle fire and the ping of ricocheting bullets echoed around the enclosure.

The prisoner's last word was, *'Missed!'*, then his head slumped lifelessly to his chest and his body fell limp.

According to prior arrangements, the corpse was immediately repatriated and several days later it was duly interred in a secluded corner of a quiet English country churchyard. Gathered at the graveside was a small band of faithful acolytes who stood facing a headstone which bore the inscription:

'NOW WHAT WAS *THAT* ALL ABOUT?'

Thus ended the life of Citizen Number One, more commonly known as 'One', the founding father of the Citizens' Revolutionary Action Party, which has an apostrophe after the *s*. One was always most particular about that.

THE BEGINNING OF THE END

One's life did not have to end in that way. Had he only kept a low profile in exile then his premature demise might easily have been avoided, but from the very outset he became a thorn in the flesh of the authorities. Within weeks of arrival in the country, he had orchestrated a common courtesy strike in which public sector workers were encouraged to go to work with a bad attitude and perform their duties in a surly and begrudging manner; but this was abandoned after only a few days when it failed to draw any attention. He later organised the peasantry into a successful boycott of Cartier, Chanel, Fabergé and other companies favoured by el Presidente.

However, it was in promoting a 'Protest rally about THIS and THAT, but mostly THAT' when he first seriously attracted the notice of the apparatchiks of the state. He was seen distributing leaflets in the streets of the capital while simultaneously whispering in people's ears. Undercover agents reported back to their superior, General Dueñas, who in turn took it to the very top.

'The Englishman enjoys a game with us, Dueñas,' said el Presidente, 'but he will soon discover that we do not play the cricket here. Cancel all police leave and call in a couple of your crack army units. We will see how he laughs when he has blood on his hands.'

On the day of the protest, the main plaza was surrounded by a cordon of police. Marksmen were strategically placed on rooftops with orders to shoot to kill at the first hint of trouble, or even without it. As the appointed hour approached, the capital was otherwise deserted. All was eerily silent and the tension in the air was palpable. In the distance, a faint clip-clopping of hooves was heard, and the louder it got the more heightened the tension became. As zero hour approached, adrenaline began to course through the veins of the policemen. Beads of sweat rolled down their faces. The snipers primed their rifles and put their eyes to the sights. Then, through the afternoon heat haze, from a side-street that fed on to the main approach to the plaza, emerged the rally—a toothless, wizened old peasant woman, leading a mangy ass by a rope with one hand, and carrying a badly translated placard in the other that read:

'KISS MY DONKEY'

El Presidente was not amused.

'He has made fools of us this time, Dueñas … but it will not happen again. Our English friend will slip up eventually and then I will have my revenge. I want him followed day and night. Nothing is to escape your notice. Do you understand?'

'Si, Presidente.'

Round-the-clock surveillance was put in place, but for some weeks there was little to report. Then came a development that had Dueñas rushing to his master.

'He has bought a truck and equipped it with a tank,' he announced.

'A tank!' exclaimed el Presidente. 'So, he plans a military coup?'

'No, no—not *that* sort of tank, Presidente—a storage container—for transporting 'goods'.'

'What sort of goods?'

Dueñas hesitated for a moment.

'Excrement, Your Excellency.'

El Presidente gave him a long, hard stare.

'You had better explain yourself, General.'

'Well, Excellency, he was observed driving from pueblo to pueblo, where he received and emptied receptacles into his mobile container in exchange for cash. When he had a full load, he was seen heading north across the border. At that point, I sent in agents to discover what was going on.'

'*And? ...*'

'And it seems that he is paying the peasants for their 'waste'—more particularly, their solid waste—their excrement.'

'Absurdo!' exclaimed el Presidente. 'Of what use is peasant poo to anyone? He is taking the fish again, Dueñas.'

'Exactly what I thought, Excellency—*at first*. But then one of his 'suppliers' let slip that the USA is embarking on an innovative renewable energy programme using human excreta as fuel. The Englishman had told him to 'keep it under his sombrero'—the information, that is—not the excrement. What is more, the concept is maybe not as crazy as it appears. After all, fortunes have been made from guano, which is used as manure. And if there is money in bird droppings ...'

'But the gringos produce their own waste ...'

'In such a country, Excellency, the diet is rich and varied. My informants tell me that our peasant produce, simple and uniform as it is, provides the ideal constituency for industrial combustibility.'

His Excellency reflected for a few moments. Then he clapped his hands and rubbed them together.

'Absolutamente! You are right, Dueñas! We will steal his thunder ... *and* his profit. Find out what he is paying and offer ten per cent more. We can drop the price again when we have squeezed him out—in fact, we can levy the waste as a household tax—on a 'pay as you go' basis, you might say.'

A few days later, to el Presidente's great satisfaction, Dueñas reported that *Uno*, as the locals called him, had been watched gesticulating wildly and remonstrating with his lost suppliers before slamming his cab door shut and driving off at great speed. Meanwhile, storage silos across the country were requisitioned and converted to purpose by government order and the construction of many more was undertaken at enormous cost to the national purse. In due course, the US ambassador was summoned to the presidential palace and, after an exchange of opening pleasantries, was invited to sit.

'I have asked you here,' explained el Presidente, 'because I have something to discuss that will be of great mutual benefit.'

The ambassador was appropriately attentive.

'The peasants here do great business and have recently been making large deposits at my bank,' continued el Presidente, smiling wryly. 'I am prepared to sell those deposits to the United States government at a very reasonable rate so that it can burn them to keep your wheels of industry turning. You might say that our *poo-poo* will help you *do-do*, if you get my meaning?'

He didn't.

El Presidente leaned in intimately towards the ambassador.

'I'm talking *shit* here,' he announced in a low, meaningful tone.

The ambassador appeared to be on the point of making a reply, but then thought better of it.

When, in the course of the ensuing conversation, it became painfully apparent to el Presidente that there had not been, was not, and would not ever likely be a human waste-based energy programme in the United States, from a mixture of embarrassment and rage his complexion changed to a bright crimson. As he left, the ambassador's face was bright crimson too, although as the result of an entirely different emotion, which he desperately tried to suppress until he was safely beyond the gates of the palace.

That was the straw which broke the camel's back. Dueñas was tasked with emptying and cleaning the silos *in person*, while One's fate was irrevocably sealed.

When One heard that a warrant had been issued for his arrest, he moved about the city disguised as a tree but, as the species wasn't indigenous to the region, he had unwittingly made himself conspicuous and was soon apprehended. With nothing on the statute books legislating against being grossly irritating, he was to be tried under the law of sedition, on the bogus charge of plotting to blow up el Presidente's zeppelin, the penalty for which was death.

The verdict was never in doubt.

'Guilty!'

And the rest, as they say, is geography.

THE BEGINNING

One did not disclose much about his personal history, but it was evident that he came from a relatively privileged background, on his mother's side at least. After a particularly satisfying meal he had been heard to exclaim, 'Just like mater's chef used to make!' His father, however, was merely a humble Church of England clergyman whose sermons were so notoriously long and dull that his church became an Anglican equivalent of Lourdes, with chronic insomniacs reputedly travelling great distances to seek a cure. They helped make up the numbers when the congregation had fallen to a critical level. The few remaining stalwarts who managed to stay conscious during the services became increasingly frustrated with their vicar and began to gently heckle him. When this failed to elicit improvement, they progressed to launching missiles in the general direction of the pulpit. It was believed to be as the result of being struck on the head by the Book of Common Prayer that he developed Tourettes Syndrome and proceeded to deliver a sermon on the —— Good Samaritan, closing with the lesson, 'Do unto others as the ——s would do unto you, the ——s'. For the next few Sundays, when word spread, he played to packed houses but, despite record attendances, the Bishop decided to remove him from his incumbency and force him into early retirement. Distraught and in despair at the ignominy of losing his parish, he made a half-hearted attempt to commit suicide by throwing himself in front of a train on a miniature railway track. He came out of it relatively unscathed, suffering only minor cuts and bruises, mostly handbag wounds from irate mothers.

Although there was never an open admission of guilt, it was suspected among his entourage that One may have initiated the school chess riots of the 1950s, when crowds of travelling supporters, adopting gang names such as the *Sophists* and *Stoics*, would rampage through towns, directing bitingly facetious remarks at locals in Latin and ancient Greek, *en passant*. It all culminated in the infamous incident in British chess history when, following a controversial 'touch-move' decision, the away fans subjected the umpire, who happened to have a pronounced eye twitch, to strains of 'The referee's a winker'. This was enough to tip the home supporters over the edge and, in the resulting melée, bishops got inserted into orifices where they had no right to be. When the dust finally settled, the floor was littered with broken national health spectacles, dental braces and brown sandals. One young man had his fingers so badly trodden on that it would be many months before he was able to play harpsichord again. It was perhaps from the horror at this carnage that One developed his doctrine of polite and non-violent protest. 'Pacifism,' he would often say, 'is the one cause worth fighting for'.

At university, One studied architecture and played an active role in student life. He called an inaugural meeting of the Society of Apathetics, which may very well have been a success had anybody bothered to show up. He also instituted the annual poetry shouting contest which was won in the first year by an entrant who delivered a superbly aggressive rendition of Shakespeare's Sonnet 18:

SHALL I COMPARE THEE TO A SUMMER'S DAY?
WELL? SHALL I, YOU TART!?

On graduation, One was articled to a local architect renowned for innovation. In an attempt to impress his employer and make a reputation in the field, he took up the challenge of building a house from the top down; but the clients unfortunately ran out of money before completion and the project was suspended indefinitely.

Disillusioned by the experience, One quit the profession and randomly decided upon a career in entertainment. Adopting the stage persona of 'The Amazing Mr Memory Loss' he toured the variety halls as an act in which he would successfully fail to answer questions from the audience. In order to heighten the drama he would strut backwards and forwards across the stage, head down in deep thought and stroking his chin.

'Don't tell me! I know this one!' he would say.

Or, 'Hang on a minute. It's on the tip of my tongue'.

Periodically he stamped his foot in frustration and let out an exasperated 'Aarrgh!'

But ultimately the answer would always elude him and he would be greeted by rapturous applause.

All went well for quite some time until one night, in a moment of complacency and forgetfulness, he accidentally remembered an answer.

When asked, 'For what was Einstein chiefly awarded the Nobel Prize in Physics?' he replied, without thinking, 'The discovery of the law of the photoelectric effect'.

There were gasps and sharp intakes of breath from the audience.

'I mean the special theory of relativity', he added hurriedly, in a desperate effort to retrieve the situation, quickly followed by 'I mean, I don't remember.'

But it was too late. He was assailed by a chorus of jeers, boos and cat-calls:

Fake!

Fraud!

Impostor!

The act had been exposed as a sham and bookings dried up overnight.

He attempted to reinvent himself as a stand-up comedian, developing jokes that were so witty and sophisticated that even the code breakers at Bletchley Park couldn't have cracked them. His routine was invariably met by a sea of stony faces. He tried explaining to the audience that his humour was indeed very funny and that they were probably not fully equipped to understand it, but it was all to no avail. The act flopped and, yet again, One found himself unemployed.

These were hungry times for One, literally. In a penniless and ravenous state, he sat down one day in an exclusive restaurant and ordered a meal for himself and another for an invisible friend called Malcolm.

'And what would sir's friend like to drink,' asked the waiter, turning and winking slyly at his colleagues.

'He's perfectly capable of choosing for himself,' said One.

'Indeed,' said the waiter, who then went through a pantomime of showing Malcolm the wine list, pointing out the merits of particular vintages, and complimenting him on his eventual choice.

When both plates and glasses were empty, and One was fully sated, he got up and casually made his way towards the door.

'Excuse me! Sir!' the waiter called after him. 'Your bill?'

'My friend's paying,' One replied, waving back towards the table.

'What friend?'

'Why, the one you discussed the wine list with, of course.'

When forced to wash the dishes, One got into such a heated spat with Malcolm over whose turn it had been to foot the bill that crockery worth more than the value of the meal got smashed.

Not long after that incident, One received his call-up papers for National Service. His family had a long-standing association with the British military. His grandfather had been shot in the Great War for refusing to desert, and his uncle had flown Wellington bombers during the Second World War until the military police eventually caught up with him.

'I'm rather busy at the moment', he told the medical officer as he sat down at the interview. 'Can't this wait until the war is over?'

'The war *is* over,' was the peevish reply.

'There you are, you see,' said One, 'you'll hardly be in need of me now'.

'And anyway,' he continued, 'I'm blind.'

He ducked as the MO threw a crumpled piece of paper at him.

'I meant *mute,*' he said, on composing himself again.

Despite being in perfect physical condition, One was nevertheless deemed unfit for national service.

Determined not to fail in life like his father, One turned his attention to politics, an occupation for which he knew that no qualifications are necessary for success other than honesty and moral integrity. It was then that he made the decision to form the Citizens' Revolutionary Action Party. For some time he was the only member, until he placed a fateful advertisement in a local newspaper.

THE BEGINNING

'TANK DRIVER WANTED
NO EXPERIENCE NECESSARY
MUST HAVE OWN TRANSPORT'

The sole respondent was the man who would become his most faithful adherent and his right-hand man—Citizen Number Two. Two turned up to the meeting in the car park of the George and Dragon pub on a bicycle.

'Where's your tank?' One asked.

'It has a flat.'

One extended his hand.

'Welcome aboard!'

Others joined the ranks in due course, although the number of active members fluctuated according to how many the medical profession considered sufficiently rehabilitated and fit for discharge, but at times crowds of several people could be mustered for demonstrations. The unofficial uniform of non-conformity at these gatherings was a black balaclava topped by a rather fetching Sunday bonnet. On one occasion the protesters stationed themselves outside Parliament Buildings where One acted as lead chanter:

ONE: What do we want?

CROWD: An end to *An Act to Attaint the Person who during the Life of the late King James, took upon him the Stile and Title of Prince of Wales and since the Decease of the said King James, hath Assumed the Name and Title of James the Third, King of England and Ireland, and James the Eighth, King of Scotland, commonly called, The Chevalier de St. George, or, The Pretender, and all his Adherents, and to give a Reward of Fifty Thousand Pounds Sterl. To any Person who shall Seize and Secure the said Pretender, if he Lands or attempts to Land in this Kingdom.*

ONE: When do we want it?
CROWD: At your convenience!

A rather embarrassed junior official eventually wandered out and had a quiet word in One's ear, to which the One responded:

'That's great news! Although I don't mean the bit about him being dead, obviously.'

Then the placards were lowered and the protestors shuffled off to the bus station.

About this time, One formed the *Purgatory's Angels,* so called because they tended to be somewhat naughty rather than very bad. They would tour the country on mopeds causing minor irritation. At transport cafés they would be a tad too noisy and leave without straightening their knives and forks or putting the chairs back under the table. When they encountered traffic wardens they would smile at them without really meaning it. In several towns they gate-crashed meetings of local debating societies and started arguments, and when chased from a village green they claimed to have thought that the 'Keep off the grass' notice was part of an anti-drugs campaign. They would ask little old ladies to help them cross the road, or send an angel along the high street to hammer on shop windows with his fists and cry desperately, 'Let me out!' In Southend-on-Sea the angels distributed 'What to see in Clacton' brochures to passengers disembarking from tourist coaches.

THE END OF THE BEGINNING

One first attracted the interest of the British security services when he wrote to the Kremlin asking for nuclear warheads to be delivered to his 3rd floor flat, adding as a post script that if he was out to leave them with his neighbour at Number 19. Then he added a second P.S. to clarify what he meant by 'delivery'.

He referred to all figures of authority as Authorized Representatives of the State, but the term was applied most particularly to the police, and his nemesis in the constabulary was Chief Superintendent Payne. When One became aware that Payne was having him tailed, he took to visiting art house cinemas where he watched foreign language films with no subtitles, or spent hours train-spotting on abandoned railway lines. At other times, he would stand at roadsides hitchhiking with a cardboard sign that read 'Nowhere', and generally didn't have to wait long for someone going his way. And when he realized that his phone was being tapped, One rang all the people he most disliked to assure them of his discretion. When they asked who he was and what he was talking about, he would declare, 'That's the spirit!', and then hang up.

As party leader, One tried to avoid politics whenever possible. He rarely proffered an opinion on political matters, but challenged on his position on unilateral disarmament he replied that it was entirely pointless unless everyone did it; and when feminists started burning their bras he was among the first to offer them support. Equality, he once said, was something that he learned at his mother's knee, but why she had it written on her knee he had no idea.

It was the ill-advised expression of an opinion that eventually forced him to skip the country. When interviewed by a particularly pretty young journalist, he incautiously remarked that the local crime lords were merely frustrated florists whose turf wars were a manifestation of peonies envy. On the evening of the day the article appeared in the newspaper he received a visit from two burly gentlemen who claimed to have a delivery from Interflora. An hour later, he was placed face down on a stretcher and taken by ambulance to A & E where he underwent an operation to have a rose removed from between his buttocks. It had been inserted stem first and was not a thornless variety. When the nurse came with a needle to administer the anaesthetic, she said, 'You may feel a bit of a prick.'

'Oh, I do!' he agreed wholeheartedly, 'Believe me, I do!'

Targeted by both state and underworld, One concluded that discretion was the better part of valour and decided to make himself scarce. On his journey to South America, he wondered why the crossing to Calais was so interminably long.

And that, dear brothers and sisters, concludes the life story of Citizen Number One, so far as we know it.

HEROES OF THE REVOLUTION

Inside One's dusty old tomes, retrieved from Two's lock-up garage in Bognor, were pages turned down at the corners, as previously mentioned, to mark certain passages relating to revolutionary characters of the past who were doubtless of great inspiration to One, and a few examples of these are included below, not least because without them this book would be even shorter than it is.

Let us begin with Count Alessandro di Cagliostro who, according to Robert Chambers in *The Book of Days*, was actually 'the son of a Pietro Balsamo, a poor shopkeeper of Palermo, and was born in 1743.' His revolutionary activities began when 'He was placed in a monastery, and being set to read the *Lives of the Saints* to the monks whilst they ate their meals, he was detected interpolating naughty fictions of his own, and was at once discharged.' Having titillated the minds of the monks, he engaged in a series of further antics, which were received with equal disapproval, and Palermo becoming too hot for him, he disappeared, eventually turning up in Rome where he met and married a girl called Lorenza, daughter of a girdle-maker. The couple assumed a variety of grandiose titles before finally settling on Count Alessandro and Countess Seraphina Cagliostro.

> In a coach-and-four they rolled through Europe, found access to the highest society, and mysteriously dispensed potions, washes, charms and love philtres. By a wine of Egypt, sold in drops more precious than nectar, they promised restoration to the vigour and beauty of youth to worn-out men and wrinkled women.

Seraphina adduced herself as a living evidence of the efficacy of the elixir. Though young and blooming, she averred she was sixty, and had a son a veteran in the Dutch service.

... which reinforces the popular notion that women do tend to lie about their age.

In the same volume is the anecdote of an unknown character who merits the title of Eater the Great:

> When Charles Gustavus, King of Sweden, was besieging Prague, a boor of a most extraordinary visage desired admittance to his tent; and being allowed to enter, he offered, by way of amusement, to devour a large hog in his presence. The old General Kœnigsmark, who stood by the King's side, hinted to his royal master that the peasant ought to be burnt as a sorcerer. "Sir," said the fellow, irritated at the remark, "if your Majesty will but make that old gentleman take off his sword and spurs, I will eat him before I begin the pig."

Of heroines of the revolution, like Countess Seraphina, there is no shortage, and credit is due to the woman who had the resourcefulness to make a living by habitually hanging herself in various parts of London. George Smeeton describes her strategy in *Doings in London*:

> In 1731, a female, of tolerable appearance, and between thirty and forty years of age, was the cause of much alarm, by pretending to *hang herself*, in different parts of the town. Her method was this: she found a convenient situation for the experiment, and suspended herself; an accomplice, always at hand for the purpose,

immediately released her from the rope, and, after rousing the neighbourhood, absconded. Humanity induced the spectators sometimes to take her into their houses, always to relieve her; who were told, when sufficiently *recovered to articulate*, that she had possessed £1500; but that, marrying an Irish captain, he robbed her of every penny, and fled; which produced despair, and a determination to commit suicide.

In the absence of further details, it can only be assumed that she was taller than average, and that if her accomplice was her husband then his dinner was always on the table in good time and to his satisfaction.

Neither has youth been lacking in inventiveness when it comes to entertaining ways in which to make one's way in the world. In the same book, Peregrine Wilson is being instructed by his guide, Mentor, on the frauds and follies practiced in London, when,

At this instant, a young lad presented himself to their notice, and asked whether they would wish to hear him "*Do* the cat's last dying speech?" Having gained their consent, the boy immediately commenced with his right hand to strike his chin with great rapidity, which, aided by his voice, produced the loud, shrill, and discordant yells of a cat, whose body, one would suppose, was jammed under the leg of a chair; and gave other proofs of his powers of imitating the feline species, truly astonishing. "That boy," said Mentor, "is named Jackson: he was taken before the magistrates at Union Hall, last year, charged, under the Vagrant Act, with sleeping in the open air. One of the constables of Lambeth stated, that on the preceding night, as he was passing along the Bishop's Walk, he heard a noise proceed from a place where timber was deposited, resembling the cries of a cat in great agony. He hastened to the spot, in order to extricate the animal, conceiving it had got jammed between the logs of wood, from its doleful lamentations. On his way thither, however, the cries of distress were changed into the most loud and boisterous squalling he ever heard in his life, as if at least a dozen cats of both sexes were engaged in their noisy amours. He therefore stopped short, not much relishing the idea of approaching too closely, snatched up a brickbat, and flung it at random (the night being too dark to discover objects) towards the place from whence the 'row' proceeded; but he might as well have spared himself the trouble, for the caterwauling, instead of diminishing, increased to a degree that was quite stunning. He therefore plucked up all his courage, and, having cautiously on tip-toe advanced, with a stone in his hand, weighty enough to knock the 'nine lives' out of any poor mouser, he was astonished, on looking about, to see no cat, or any thing in the shape of a cat, but discovered the boy Jackson, lying very comfortably coiled up between two immense beams of timber. He pretended to be asleep at first, but when the constable said he was convinced he was only shamming, and added, that the uproar the cats had been making would have prevented any human being from closing his eyes, 'the boy then admitted,' said the constable, 'to my wonderment, that it was he who had kicked up the disturbance, and imitated the cats to the very life. And so,' added the constable, 'I took him to the watchouse, and locked him up, for lying out in the open air.'"

"The boy, who stood smiling during the constable's statement of his adventures the night before, on being asked how he got his livelihood, replied, 'By chanting the cat's last dying speech.' The magistrates discharged him, after admonishing him not to be found sleeping again in the open air."

From *Books Fatal to their Authors* we learn of Quirinus Kuhlmann who believed himself to be the Son of God, but often found difficulty in convincing others, and was not infrequently obliged to leave countries without being afforded ample opportunity to pack:

He then proceeded to Turkey on his mission, and presented himself to the Sultan. Although ignorant of the language of the country, he persuaded himself that he could speak in any tongue; but when they led him into the presence of the Sultan he waited in vain for the burning words of eloquence to flow. The Turks dealt with him according to his folly, and bestowed on him a sound thrashing.

In *The Complete Newgate Calendar* is told the tale of William Nevison, 'A highwayman who, dying of the plague as was thought, reappeared as his own ghost, and was finally executed at York in 1684.'

Committing some robberies in Leicestershire, he was there taken, and committed to Leicester Jail, where he was so narrowly watched, and strongly ironed, that he could scarce stir; yet by a cunning stratagem he procured his enlargement before the assizes came. For one day, feigning himself extremely ill, he sent for two or three trusty friends, one of whom was a physician, who gave out that he was sick of a pestilential fever; and that unless he had the benefit of some open air, in some chamber, he would certainly infect the whole jail, and die of the said distemper. Hereupon the jailer takes off his fetters and removes him into another room, to lie by himself. In the meantime a nurse was provided him, and his physician came twice or thrice a day to visit him, who gave out there was no hopes of his life, and that his distemper was extremely contagious. On which report, the jailer's wife would not let her husband, nor any of the servants, go nearer than the door; which gave Nevison's confederates a full liberty to practise their intent, which they did thus. A painter was one day brought in, who made all over his breast blue spots, resembling those that are the forerunners of death in the disease commonly called the plague; as likewise several marks on his hands, face and body, which are usually on such that so die. All which being done, the physician prepared a dose whereby his spirits were confined for the space of an hour or two, and then immediately gave out that he was dead. Hereupon his friends demand his body, bringing a coffin to carry him away in. The jailer, as customary, orders a jury—the nurse having formally laid him out—to examine the cause of his death, who, fearing the contagion he was said to die of, stayed not long to consider thereon; but having viewed him, seeing the spots and marks of death about him, his eyes set, and his jaws close muffled, they brought in their verdict that he died of the plague; and thereupon he was put in the coffin and carried off.

Back on the road again, Nevison continued in his chosen profession, leaving some victims in the difficult position of deciding whether or not to report being robbed by a ghost.

In the third volume of *Duffy's Hibernian Magazine* of 1861 we encounter an Irish revolutionary who comes to the aid of a group of English visitors to the Sugar Loaf mountain in County Wicklow.

> The tourists, it appeared, had determined on making the ascent of the Great Sugar Loaf, and had with them a hamper well stored with creature comforts; so well stored, indeed, that the weight of it was to the short-winded Saxons a subject much more pleasant to contemplate than to experience.
>
> They, nevertheless, attempted the ascent, carrying the precious freight as best they could, but the day was intensely hot, and they were making but little way, growing more and more troubled every minute, when a fine specimen of a native, who sometimes acted as a local guide, appeared upon the scene. A bargain was soon made, that for the sum of two and sixpence the newcomer should shoulder the source of their present trouble, and, as they fondly imagined, future enjoyment, and convey it to the very summit of the mountain. The simple peasant guide seemed greatly to pity the inexperience, as mountaineers, of his now rather jaded employers, and with admirable consideration directed them by a route which, though somewhat longer, was less abruptly steep than that by which he himself should go. Few of our readers, we are sure, have not sometime or other experienced the effect of keen mountain air on their appetites, particularly after a long dusty summer day's drive, and not a little pedestrian exercise.

We may imagine, then, the visions of edibles and potables which floated upon the imaginations of the climbers, for had they not clubbed for the contents of the precious basket, and did they not each and all know to an ounce what was to be expected. On and on they went, getting every moment more desperate at the length of the journey and the steepness of the hill; but it was pleasant to see the guide doing his duty manfully, though even he seemed to suffer somewhat under the weight of his burden. He was not always visible, however, but then he would reappear from behind some rock, steadily working skyward, as if *"excelsior"* had been his motto.

At length, having reached to within about twenty yards of the summit, he rests the basket on the rock, and throws himself beside it with the air of one completely exhausted. The tourists presently gather round, and the poor fellow, in piteous accents, begs that their honours will convey his late burden the few yards farther it has to go themselves, as "he feels it coming on him, and he must hasten home, where he will have Judy to mind him."

"What's coming on?—what's the matter?" they exclaimed.

"Why, then, your honours, it's the falling-sickness, that sometimes attacks me after I do be hard worked on a hot day like this, God bless it, and I feel just as if the fit was coming on now, and surely, gentlemen, 'twould only be a Christian act of kindness to let me go home, and to take the basket the few yards yourselves."

"All right," says one of the Englishmen; "here is your money, my man, and you had better get along home as quickly as possible: we shall be hard set, I dare say, to carry ourselves down over these cursed rocks, which roll about so under one, without having also to carry a man in a fit."

"Long life to your honour. I'll not lose a minute," said the fellow, slowly disappearing.

Ten minutes or so brought our hungry, thirsty, puffing, but delighted party to the long-wished-for spot on the very highest peak of the mountain, and a drink was instantaneously proposed by each individual. A few cords are cut, the lid opens, the cloth is removed, and, O heavens! judge of their feelings to find that the basket they had so painfully carried contained nothing but stones—granite stones!

At another time, in another place, our guide might have been hailed as a maker of miracles, albeit not as practical and popular as turning water into wine; but prophets are often despised in their own country, so, instead, he was invited to spend some time in Wicklow jail.

Let us finish with a couple of headstone inscriptions from *Antiente Epitaphes* compiled by Thomas Ravenshaw, the first being for Mary Ford at Potterne, Wiltshire, in 1790:

> Here lyes MARY the Wife of JOHN FORD,
> We hope her soule is gone to the LORD;
> But if for Hell she has chang'd this life,
> She had better be there than John Ford's wife.

And, finally, one from 1797 for William Ash of West Down, Devon:

> Reader, pass on, nor waste your precious time
> On bad biography and murdered rhyme:
> What I was before 's well known to my neighbours,
> What I am now is no concern of yours.

www.ingramcontent.com/pod-product-compliance
Lightning Source LLC
Chambersburg PA
CBHW060552030426
42337CB00019B/3528